"Father, Forgive Them For They Know Not What They Do."

(Luke 23:34)

*Meditations on the First Word
from the Cross*

Archbishop Fulton J. Sheen

Copyright © 2021 by Al Smith

Printed in the United States of America. All rights reserved.

Cover design by Janicka Barman www.twitter.com/barman_janika

On the cover: Jesus and the Two Thieves (2008) painting by Michael D. O'Brien © Michael D. O'Brien.

Scripture quotations are taken from the Douay-Rheims edition of the Old and New Testaments.

No part of this book may be reproduced, stored in a retrieval system, or transmitted in any form, or by any means, electronic, mechanical, photocopying, or otherwise, without the prior written permission of the publisher, except by a reviewer, who may quote brief passages in a review.

Bishop Sheen Today
280 John Street
Midland, Ontario, Canada
L4R 2J5

www.bishopsheentoday.com

Library of Congress Cataloging-in-Publication Data

Names: Sheen, Fulton J. (Fulton John), 1895-1979, author. | Smith, Al (Allan J.), editor. | Sheen, Fulton J. (Fulton John), 1895-1979. Cross and the Beatitudes. | Sheen, Fulton J. (Fulton John), 1895-1979. Rainbow of sorrow. | Sheen, Fulton J. (Fulton John), 1895-1979. Seven last words. | Sheen, Fulton J. (Fulton John), 1895-1979. Seven virtues. | Sheen, Fulton J. (Fulton John), 1895-1979. Seven words of Jesus and Mary. | Sheen, Fulton J. (Fulton John), 1895-1979. Seven words to the Cross. | Sheen, Fulton J. (Fulton John), 1895-1979. Victory over vice. | Sheen, Fulton J. (Fulton John), 1895-1979. Cross and the Beatitudes.

Title: Father, Forgive Them For They Know Not What They Do: Meditations on the First Word from the Cross / Archbishop Fulton J. Sheen: compiled by Al Smith.

Description: Midland, Ontario: Bishop Sheen Today Publishing, 2021. | Includes bibliographical references.

Identifiers: paperback ISBN 978-1-990427-34-3 /
e-Book ISBN 978-1-6990427-35-0 /

Subjects: LCSH: Jesus Christ — Seven last words.

First printing

J.M.J.

To Our Lady, Seat of Wisdom,
In Humble Petition That,
Through The Immaculate Heart Of Mary,
The World May Find Its Way Back To
The Sacred Heart of Jesus

Ad Maiorem Dei Gloriam
Inque Hominum Salutem

The Seven Last Words of Christ

The First Word
"Father, Forgive Them For They Know Not What They Do."

The Second Word
"This Day Thou Shalt Be With Me In Paradise."

The Third Word
"Woman, Behold Thy Son; Behold Thy Mother."

The Fourth Word
"My God! My God! Why Hast Thou Forsaken Me?"

The Fifth Word
"I Thirst."

The Sixth Word
"It Is Finished."

The Seventh Word
"Father, Into Thy Hands I Commend My Spirit."

Contents

Introduction

First Meditation
          Father, Forgive Them For They Know Not What They Do

Second Meditation
          Our Father Who Art In Heaven

Third Meditation
          The Confiteor

Fourth Meditation
          Blessed Are The Meek

Fifth Meditation
          Unjust Suffering

Sixth Meditation
          Anger

Seventh Meditation
          Fortitude

Eighth Meditation
          A Word To Humanists

Ninth Meditation
          The Value Of Ignorance

Acknowledgments

About the Author

Introduction

I have learned more from the crucifix than from any book.

St. Thomas Aquinas

Archbishop Fulton J. Sheen was a man for all seasons. Over his lifetime, he spent himself for souls, transforming lives with the clear teaching of the truths of Christ and His Church through his books, his radio addresses, his lectures, his television series, and his many newspaper columns.

The topics of this much-sought-after lecturer ranged from the social concerns of the day to matters of faith and morals. With an easy and personable manner, Sheen could strike up a conversation on just about any subject, making numerous friends as well as converts.

During the 1930s and '40s, Fulton Sheen was the featured speaker on The Catholic Hour radio broadcast, and millions of listeners heard his radio addresses each week. His topics ranged from politics and the economy to philosophy and man's eternal pursuit of happiness.

Along with his weekly radio program, Sheen wrote dozens of books and pamphlets. One can safely say that through his writings, thousands of people changed their perspective about God and the Church. Sheen was quoted as saying, "There are not one hundred people in the United States who hate the Catholic Church, but there are millions who hate what they wrongly perceive the Catholic Church to be."

Possessing a burning zeal to dispel the myths about Our Lord and His Church, Sheen gave a series of powerful presentations on Christ's Passion and His seven last words from the Cross. As a Scripture scholar,

Archbishop Sheen knew full well the power contained in preaching Christ crucified. With St. Paul, he could say, "For I decided to know nothing among you except Jesus Christ and him crucified" (1 Cor. 2:2).

During his last recorded Good Friday address in 1979, Archbishop Sheen spoke of having given this type of reflection on the subject of Christ's seven last words from the cross "for the fifty-eighth consecutive time." Whether from the young priest in Peoria, Illinois, the university professor in Washington, D.C., or the bishop in New York, Sheen's messages were sure to make an indelible mark on his listeners.

Given their importance and the impact they had on society, it seemed appropriate to bring together in this anthology some of Archbishop Sheen's meditations on the Seven Last Words Our Blessed Lord spoke from the Cross on Calvary.

The meditations contained in this book are taken from several books and articles written by Sheen between 1933 and 1945.

The Seven Last Words. (New York: Century, 1933)
The Seven Last Words and the Our Father. (Huntington, Indiana: Our Sunday Visitor 1935)
Calvary and the Mass. (New York: P. J. Kenedy and Sons, 1936)
The Cross and the Beatitudes. (New York: P. J. Kenedy and Sons, 1937)
The Rainbow of Sorrow. (New York: P. J. Kenedy and Sons, 1938)
Victory over Vice. (New York: P. J. Kenedy and Sons, 1939)
The Seven Virtues. (New York: P. J. Kenedy and Sons, 1940)
Seven Words to the Cross. (New York: P. J. Kenedy and Sons, 1944)
Seven Words of Jesus and Mary. (New York: P. J. Kenedy and Sons, 1945)

These mediations have been selected to provide nine unique reflections for study and meditation on the Seven Last Words.

First Meditation - A reflection on the words spoken by Christ from the Cross.
Second Meditation – A reflection on a passage from the Lord's Prayer.
Third Meditation – A reflection on a part of the Mass.
Fourth Meditation – A reflection on one of the Beatitudes.
Fifth Meditation – A reflection about sorrow and suffering.
Sixth Meditation – A reflection addressing one of the seven deadly sins.
Seventh Meditation – A reflection on the virtues.
Eighth Meditation – A reflection on dealing with individuals who reject the Church and Christ's teachings.
Ninth Meditation – A reflection on the unity of Jesus and Mary.

As the reader ponders these reflections, they might have to pause for a moment or two over a sentence that is full of deep meaning that stirs the heart. He might also find that Archbishop Sheen has repeated certain lines throughout these reflections to drive home a point or an important theme, as any good teacher would do.

On October 2, 1979, when visiting St. Patrick's Cathedral in New York City, Pope John Paul II embraced Fulton Sheen and spoke into his ear a blessing and an affirmation. He said: "You have written and spoken well of the Lord Jesus Christ. You are a loyal son of the Church."

On the day Archbishop Sheen died (December 9, 1979), he was found in his private chapel before the Eucharist in the shadow of the cross. Archbishop Sheen was a man purified in the fires of love and by the wood of the Cross.

It is hoped that, upon reading these reflections, the reader will concur with the heartfelt affirmation given by St. John Paul II and countless others of Sheen's wisdom and fidelity. May these writings by Archbishop Fulton J. Sheen evoke a greater love and appreciation for the Church, the Passion of Lord Jesus Christ, and the need for us to look into our souls each day.

Archbishop Sheen's dynamic personality combined with his brilliant mind, tireless pen, and eloquent voice has made him one of the best-known figures in the world. His radio and television appearances have been phenomenally successful and are still viewed today. His books and magazine articles continue to gratify and attract a boundless circle of readers. This collection of meditations gives still another example of why this continues to be so today.

First Meditation

Father, Forgive Them, For They Know Not What They Do.

It seems to be a fact of human psychology that when death approaches, the human heart speaks its words of love to those whom it holds closest and dearest. There is no reason to suspect that it is otherwise in the case of the Heart of hearts. If He spoke in a graduated order to those whom He loved most, then we may expect to find in His first three words the order of His love and affection. His first words went out to enemies: "Father, forgive them," His second to sinners: "This day you will be with Me in Paradise," and His third to saints: "Woman, behold your son." Enemies, sinners, and saints -- such is the order of Divine Love and Thoughtfulness.

The congregation anxiously awaited His first word. The executioners expected Him to cry, for everyone pinned on the gibbet of the Cross had done it before Him. Seneca tells us that those who were crucified cursed the day of their birth, the executioners, their mothers, and even spat on those who looked upon them. Cicero tells us that at times it was necessary to cut out the tongues of those who were crucified, to stop their terrible blasphemies. Hence the executioners expected a cry but not the kind of cry that they heard. The scribes and Pharisees expected a cry, too, and they were quite sure that He who had preached "Love your enemies," and "Do good to them that hate you," would now forget that Gospel with the piercing of feet and hands. They felt that the excruciating and agonizing pains would scatter to the winds any resolution He might have taken to keep up appearances. Everyone expected a cry, but no one with the exception of the three at the foot of the Cross expected the cry they did hear. Like some fragrant trees which bathe in perfume the very axe which gnashes them, the great Heart on the Tree of Love poured out from its depths something less a cry than a prayer, the soft, sweet, low prayer of pardon and forgiveness: "Father, forgive them, for they know not what they do."

Forgive whom? Forgive enemies? The soldier in the court-room of Caiaphas who struck Him with a mailed fist; Pilate, the politician, who condemned a God to retain the friendship of Caesar; Herod, who robed Wisdom in the garment of a fool; the soldiers who swung the King of Kings on a tree between heaven and earth -- forgive them? Forgive them, why? Because they know what they do? No, because they know not what they do. If they knew what they were doing and still went on doing it; if they knew what a terrible crime they were committing by sentencing Life to death; if they knew what a perversion of justice it was to choose Barabbas to Christ; if they knew what cruelty it was to take the feet that trod everlasting hills and pinion them to the limb of a tree; if they knew what they were doing and still went on doing it, unmindful of the fact that the very blood which they shed was capable of redeeming them, they would never be saved! Why, they would be damned if it were not for the fact that they were ignorant of the terrible thing they did when they crucified Christ! It was only the ignorance of their great sin that brought them within the pale of the hearing of that cry from the Cross. It is not wisdom that saves; it is ignorance!

There is no redemption for the fallen angels. Those great spirits headed by the Bearer of Light, Lucifer, endowed with an intelligence compared with which ours is but that of a child, saw the consequences of each of their decisions just as clearly as we see that two and two make four. Having made a decision, they made it irrevocably; there was no taking it back, and hence there was no future redemption. It is because they knew what they were doing that they were excluded from the hearing of that cry that went forth from the Cross. It is not wisdom that saves; it is ignorance!

In like manner, if we knew what a terrible thing sin was and went on sinning; if we knew how much love there was in the Incarnation and still refused to nourish ourselves with the Bread of Life; if we knew how much sacrificial love there was in the Sacrifice of the Cross and still refused to fill the chalice of our heart with that love; if we knew how much mercy there was in the Sacrament of Penance, and still refused to bend a humble knee to a hand that had the power to loose both in heaven and on earth; if we knew how much life there was in the Eucharist and still refused to take of the Bread which makes life everlasting and still refused to drink of that Wine that produces and enriches virgins; if we knew all the truth there is in the Church as the mystical body of Christ and still turned our backs to it like other Pilates; if we knew all these things and still stayed away from Christ and His Church, we should be lost! It is not wisdom that saves; it is ignorance! It is only our ignorance of how good God is that excuses us for not being saints!

PRAYER

Dear Jesus! I do not want to know the wisdom of the world; I do not want to know on whose anvil snow-flakes are hammered or the hiding-place of darkness or from whose womb came the ice, or why the gold falls to the earth earthly, and fire climbs to the heavens heavenly; I do not want to know literature and science, or the four-dimensional universe in which we live; I do not want to know the length of the universe in terms of light years; I do not want to know the breadth of the earth as it dances about the chariot of the sun; I do not want to know the heights of the stars, chaste candles of the night; I do not want to know the depths of the sea or the secrets of its watery palace. I want to be ignorant of all these things. I want only to know the length, the breadth, the height and the depth of Thy redeeming Love on the Cross, Sweet Saviour of Men. I want to be ignorant of everything in the world -- everything but You, dear Jesus. And then, by the strangest of strange paradoxes, I shall be wise!

The Seven Last Words, 1933

Second Meditation

Our Father Who Art In Heaven

"Our Father Who art in heaven."

"Father, forgive them for they know not what they do."

The first petition of the Our Father Our Lord taught us was the prayer of priestly intercession: "Our Father Who art in heaven." The first word from the Cross was the intercessory prayer of the perfect Priest: "Father forgive them for they know not what they do."

The Priest whence all priesthood is derived once asked us to look up to our Father Who is in Heaven. Now He begs that same Father to blot out the sins of those who crucify Him and to forgive them "for they know not what they do." He was finding an excuse for sins. He was telling His Father that we crucified Him only because of our ignorance. If we knew what we were doing, we would never have denied the Father in Heaven. Salvation is possible only because of our ignorance of how good God the Father is to send His only begotten Son into the world that we might have life in His name.

When our enemies crucify us, we say: "They should have known better." When we crucified Him, He said: "Forgive them, for they know not what they do." We love those who love us and honor those who flatter us; He loved those who hated Him and forgave even the hands that drove the nails. He loves not only the lovable, as we do – He also loves the hateful, which we are. That is why there is hope for us! Our Father Who art in heaven, forgive us for we know not what we do".

The Seven Last Words and the Our Father, 1935

Third Meditation

The Confiteor

"Father, forgive them, for they know not what they do."

The Mass begins with the Confiteor. The Confiteor is a prayer in which we confess our sins and ask the Blessed Mother and the saints to intercede to God for our forgiveness, for only the clean of heart can see God. Our Blessed Lord too begins His Mass with the Confiteor. But His Confiteor differs from ours in this: He has no sins to confess. He is God and therefore is sinless. "Which of you shall convince me of sin?" His Confiteor then cannot be a prayer for the forgiveness of *His* sins; but it can be a prayer for the forgiveness of *our* sins.

Others would have screamed, cursed, wrestled, as the nails pierced their hands and feet. But no vindictiveness finds place in the Saviour's breast; no appeal comes from His lips for vengeance on His murderers; He breathes no prayer for strength to bear His pain. Incarnate Love forgets injury, forgets pain, and in that moment of concentrated agony reveals something of the height, the depth, and the breadth of the wonderful love of God, as He says His Confiteor: "Father, forgive them, for they know not what they do."

He did not say "Forgive Me," but "Forgive them." The moment of death was certainly the one most likely to produce confession of sin, for conscience in the last solemn hours does assert its authority; and yet not a single sigh of penitence escaped His lips. He was associated with sinners, but never associated with sin. In death as well as life, He was unconscious of a single unfulfilled duty to His heavenly Father. And why? Because a sinless Man is not just a man; He is more than mere man. He is sinless, because He is God -- and there is the difference. We draw our prayers from the depths of our consciousness of sin: He drew His silence from His own intrinsic sinlessness. That one word "Forgive" proves Him to be the Son of God.

Notice the grounds on which He asked His heavenly Father to forgive us -- "Because they know not what they do." When anyone injures us, or blames us wrongly, we say: "They should have known better." But when we sin against God, He finds an excuse for forgiveness -- our ignorance.

There is no redemption for the fallen angels. The blood drops that fell from the cross on Good Friday in that Mass of Christ did not touch the spirits of the fallen angels. Why? Because they knew what they were doing? They saw all the consequences of their acts, just as clearly as we see that two and two make four, or that a thing cannot exist and not exist at the same time. Truths of this kind when understood cannot be taken back; they are irrevocable and eternal. Hence when they decided to rebel against Almighty God, there was no taking back the decision. They *knew* what they were doing!

But with us it is different. We do not see the consequences of our acts as clearly as the angels; we are weaker, we are ignorant. But if we did know that every sin of pride wove a crown of thorns for the head of Christ; if we knew that every contradiction of His divine command made for Him the sign of contradiction, the Cross; if we knew that every grasping avaricious act nailed His hands, and every journey into the byways of sin dug His feet; if we knew how good God is and still went on sinning, we would never be saved. It is only our ignorance of the infinite love of the Sacred Heart that brings us within the hearing of His Confiteor from the Cross: "Father, forgive them, for they know not what they do."

These words, let it be deeply graven on our souls, do not constitute an *excuse* for continued sin, but a *motive* for contrition and penance. Forgiveness is not a denial of sin. Our Lord does not *deny* the horrible fact of sin, and that is where the modern world is wrong. It explains sin away: it ascribes it to a fall in the evolutionary process, to a survival of ancient taboos; it identifies it with psychological verbiage.

In a word, the modern world *denies* sin. Our Lord reminds us that it is the most terrible of all realities. Otherwise why does it give Sinlessness a cross? Why does it shed innocent blood? Why does it have such awful associations: blindness, compromise, cowardice, hatred, and cruelty? Why does it now lift itself out of the realm of the impersonal and assert itself as personal by nailing Innocence to a gibbet? An abstraction cannot do that. But sinful man can.

Hence He, who loved men unto death, allowed sin to wreak its vengeance upon Him, in order that they might forever understand its horror as the crucifixion of Him who loved them most.

There is no denial of sin here -- and yet, with all its horror, the Victim forgives. In that one and the same event, there is the sign of sin's utter depravity and the seal of divine forgiveness. From that point on, no man can look upon a crucifix and say that sin is not serious, nor can he ever say that it cannot be forgiven. By the way He suffered, He revealed the reality of sin; by the way He bore it, He shows His mercy toward the sinner.

It is the Victim who has suffered that forgives: and in that combination of a Victim so humanly beautiful, so divinely loving, so wholly innocent, does one find a Great Crime and a Greater Forgiveness. Under the shelter of the Blood of Christ the worst sinners may take their stand; for there is a power in that Blood to turn back the tides of vengeance which threaten to drown the world.

The world will give you sin explained away, but only on Calvary do you experience the divine contradiction of sin forgiven. On the Cross, supreme self-giving and divine love transforms sin's worst act in the noblest deed and sweetest prayer the world has ever seen or heard, the Confiteor of Christ: "Father, forgive them, for they know not what they do."

That word "Forgive," which rang out from the Cross that day when sin rose to its full strength and then fell defeated by Love, did not die with its echo. Not long before, that same merciful Saviour had taken means to prolong forgiveness through space and time, even to the consummation of the world. Gathering the nucleus of His Church round about Him, He said to His Apostles: "Whose sins you shall forgive, they are forgiven."

Somewhere in the world today then, the successors of the Apostles have the power to forgive. It is not for us to ask: But how can man forgive sins? -- for man cannot forgive sins. But God can forgive sins *through* man, for is not that the way God forgave His executioners on the cross, namely through the instrumentality of His human nature?

Why then is it not reasonable to expect Him still to forgive sins through other human natures to whom He gave that power? And where find those human natures?

You know the story of the box, which was long ignored and even ridiculed as worthless; and one day it was opened and found to contain the great heart of a giant. In every Catholic Church that box exists. We call it the confessional box. It is ignored and ridiculed by many, but in it is to be found the Sacred Heart of the forgiving Christ forgiving sinners through the uplifted hand of His priest as He once forgave through His own uplifted hands on the Cross. There is only one forgiveness -- the Forgiveness of God. There is only one "Forgive" -- the "Forgive" of an eternal Divine Act in which we come in contact at various moments of time.

As the air is always filled with symphony and speech, but we do not hear it unless we tune it in on our radios, so neither do souls feel the joy of that eternal and divine "Forgive" unless they are attuned to it in time; and the confessional box is the place where we tune in to that cry from the Cross.

Would to God that our modern mind instead of denying the guilt, would look to the Cross, admit its guilt, and seek forgiveness; would that those who have uneasy consciences that worry them in the light, and haunt them in the darkness, would seek relief, not on the plane of medicine but on the plane of Divine Justice; would that they who tell the dark secrets of their minds, would do so not for the sake of sublimation, but for the sake of purgation; would that those poor mortals who shed tears in silence would find an absolving hand to wipe them away.

Must it be forever true that the greatest tragedy of life is not what happens to souls, but rather what souls miss. And what greater tragedy is there than to miss the peace of sin forgiven? The Confiteor is at the foot of the altar our cry of unworthiness: the Confiteor from the Cross is our hope of pardon and absolution. The wounds of the Saviour were terrible, but the worst wound of all would be to be unmindful that we caused it all. The Confiteor can save us from that, for it is an admission that there is something to be forgiven -- and more than we shall ever know.

There is a story told of a nun who was one day dusting a small image of our Blessed Lord in the chapel. In the course of her duty, she let it slip to the floor. She picked it up undamaged, she kissed it, and put it back again in its place, saying, "If you had never fallen, you never would have received that." I wonder if our Blessed Lord does not feel the same way about us, for if we had never sinned, we never could call Him "Saviour."

Calvary And The Mass, 1936

Fourth Meditation

Blessed Are The Meek

"Blessed are the meek: for they shall possess the land."

"Father, forgive them, for they know not what they do."

Our Blessed Lord began His public life on the Mount of the Beatitudes, by preaching: "Blessed are the meek: for they shall possess the land." He finished his public life on the Hill of Calvary by practicing that meekness: "Father, forgive them, for they know not what they do."

How different this is from the beatitude of the world! The world blesses not the meek, but the vindictive; it praises not the one who turns the other cheek, but the one who renders evil for evil; it exalts not the humble, but the aggressive. Communism has carried that spirit of violence, class-struggle, and the clenched fist to an extreme the like of which the world before has never seen.

To correct such a war-like attitude of the clenched fist, Our Lord both *preached* and *practiced* meekness.

He preached it in those memorable words that continue the Beatitudes: "You have heard that it hath been said: An eye for an eye, and a tooth for a tooth. But I say to you not to resist evil: but if one strike thee on thy right cheek, turn to him also the other: and if a man will contend with thee in judgment, and take away thy coat, let go thy cloak also unto him. And whosoever shall force thee one mile, go with him other two. ... You have heard that it hath been said: Thou shalt love your neighbor, and hate thy enemy. But I say to you: Love your enemies: do good to them that hate you: and pray for them that persecute and calumniate you that you may be the children of your Father who is in heaven, who maketh His sun to rise upon the good and bad, and raineth upon the just and the unjust. For if you love them that love you, what reward shall you have? do not even the publicans do this? And if you salute your brethren only, what do you more? do not also the heathens this? Be you therefore perfect, as also your heavenly Father is perfect."

But He not only preached meekness; He *practiced* it. When His own people picked up stones to throw at Him, He threw none back in return; when His fellow townsmen brought Him to the brow of the hill to cast Him over the precipice, He walked through their midst unharmed; when the soldier struck Him with a mailed fist, and made the Saviour feel by anticipation the clenched fist of Communism He answered meekly: "If I have spoken evil, give testimony of the evil: but if well, why strikest thou me."

When they swore to kill Him, He did not use His power to strike dead even a single enemy; and now on the Cross, meekness reaches its peak, when to those who dig the Hands which feed the world, and to those who pierce the Feet which shepherd souls, He pleads: "Father, forgive them, for they know not what they do."

Which is right -- the violence of Communism or the meekness of Christ? Communism says meekness is weakness. But that is because it does not understand the meaning of Christian meekness. Meekness is not cowardice; meekness is not an easy-going temperament, sluggish and hard to arouse; meekness is not a spineless passivity which allows everyone to walk over us. No! Meekness is self-possession. That is why the reward of meekness is possession.

A weak person can never be meek, because he is never self-possessed; meekness is that virtue which controls the combative, violent, and pugnacious powers of our nature, and is therefore the best and noblest road to self-realization.

The meek man is not a man who refuses to fight, nor is he a man who will never become angry. A meek man is a man who will never do one thing: he will never fight when his conceit is attacked, but only when a principle is at stake. And there is the keynote to the difference of the anger of the Communist and the anger of the meek man.

Communism begins at the moment conceit is attacked; fist clenched and rise as soon as the ego is challenged; cheeks flush as soon as self-love is wounded, and blood boils and flows at that split second when pride is humbled.

The anger of the Communist is based on selfishness; he hates the rich not because he loves the poor in spirit, but because he wants to be rich himself. Every Communist is really a capitalist without any cash in his pockets. Selfishness is the world's greatest sin; that is why the world hates those who hate it, why it is jealous of those who have more; why it is envious of those who do more; why it dislikes those who refuse to flatter, and why it scorns those who tell us the truth about ourselves; its whole life is inspired by the egotistical, and the personal, and its wrath is born of that self-love.

Now consider the anger of the meek man. For the meek man, not selfishness but righteousness is his guiding principle. He is so possessed, he never allows his fists to go up for an unholy purpose, or in defense of his pride or vanity, or conceit, or because he wants the wealth of another. Only the principles of God's righteousness arouse a meek man. Moses was a meek man, but he broke the tablets of stone when he found his people were disobeying God.

Our Lord is Meekness itself, and yet He drove the buyers and sellers from the Temple when they prostituted His Father's House; but when He came to the doves, He was so self-possessed He gently released them from the cages. He is so much master of Himself, that He is angry only when holiness is attacked, but never when His Person is attacked. That is why when the Gerasenes besought Our Lord to leave their coasts, without a single retort, "entering into a boat, He passed over the water and came into His own city."

That is why when men laughed Him to scorn He said nothing but approached the dead daughter of Jairus, and went on His work of mercy, oblivious to their insults, and restored her to life. That is why He addressed Judas as "Friend" when he blistered his lips with a kiss. That is why Our Lord from the Cross prays for the forgiveness of His enemies. Their wrath directed against His Body He would not return, though He might have smitten them all dead by the power of His Divinity. Rather, He forgave them, for "they know not what they do."

If ever innocence had a right to protest against injustice, it was in the case of Our Lord. And yet he extends pardon. Their insults to His Person, He ignores. Had He not preached meekness? Now must He not practice it?

And how could He practice it better than to pray for those who were crucifying him? And what greater meekness could there be than to excuse them because they knew not what they did. What a lesson for us to remember: that those who do us harm, may, too, be of the same type of misguided consciences as those who crucified Christ?

From that dread day on, there have been two motives for withdrawing from battle: either because we are afraid or because we are husbanding our energies for a more important battle. The second kind is the meekness of Our Lord.

Be not angry, then, when your conceit is attacked. It will do no harm. As Our Lord reminds us: "Blessed are they that suffer persecution for justice's sake; for theirs is the kingdom of heaven."

In contrast to this Christian philosophy of forgiveness, there exist for the first time in the history of the world a philosophy and a political and social system based not on love, but on hate, and that is Communism. Communism believes that the only way it can establish itself is by inciting revolution, class-struggle, and violence. Hence its regime is characterized by a hatred of those who believe the family is the basic unit of society. The very Communistic gesture of the clenched fist is a token of its pugnacious and destructive spirit, and a striking contrast indeed to the nailed hand of the Saviour pleading forgiveness for the clenched-fisted generation who sent Him to the Cross.

It is startling indeed to recall that we followers of Our Lord believe in violence just as much as do the Communists. Has not Our Lord said: "the kingdom of heaven suffereth violence, and the violent bear it away." But here is the difference: Communists believe in violence to one's neighbor; we believe in violence to ourselves. Communists struggle against all who refuse to have the same hate; we struggle against ourselves, our lower passions, our concupiscence, our selfishness, our egotism, our sensuality, and our meanness -- in a word, against all that prevents us from realizing the best and highest things in our nature. Communism crucifies its enemies; we crucify that which makes us think anyone is our enemy. Communism hates the love of Christians; we hate that which makes us hate Communists. If Communists used as much violence on their selfishness as they use on others, they would all be saints!

Their hatred is weakness, for it refuses to see that collective selfishness is just as wrong as individual selfishness; it is the weakness of the man who is not self-possessed, who uses his fist instead of his mind, who resorts to violence for the same reason the ignorant man resorts to blasphemy; namely, because he has not sufficient intellectual strength to express himself otherwise.

What, then, must be our attitude toward the hatred Communists bear to us? It must be the attitude of the Holy Father who asked us to pray for the *Communists*. It must be the attitude of those Spanish priests who before being shot by the Communists asked them to kneel down and receive their blessing and their forgiveness. And what is this but a reflection of Our Lord's attitude on the Cross: meekness, love, and forgiveness?

What must be our attitude toward *Communism*? We must possess a strength, a force, and a daring which exposes its errors and goes down to death on the Cross rather than accept the least of its principles of hate.

They will not love us for our meekness, and it will be hard for us not to be angry when our conceit and our pride, and possibly our possessions, are attacked; but there is no escaping the Divine injunction: Blessed are ye when they shall revile you, and persecute you, and speak all that is evil against you, untruly, for my sake: Be glad and rejoice for your reward is very great in heaven". "If the world hate you, know ye that it has hated me before you. If you had been of the world, the world would love its own; but because you are not of the world, but I have chosen you out of the world, therefore the world hateth you". "The hour cometh that whosoever killeth you will think that he doth a service to God."

If then we have enemies, let us forgive them. If we suffer unjustly, then we can practice the virtue of charity. If we suffer justly, and we probably do, for we have sins to atone for, then we can practice the virtue of justice.

What right have we to hate others, since our own selfishness is often the cause of their hatred? The first word from the Cross and the Beatitude of meekness both demand that we tear up self-love by the roots; love our executioners; forgive them, for they know not what they do; do a favor for those who insult us; be kind to the thieves who accuse us of theft; be forgiving to liars who denounce us for lying; be charitable to the adulterers who charge us with impurity.

Be glad and rejoice for their hate. It will only harm our pride, but not our character; it will cauterize our conceit, but not blemish our soul -- for the very insult of the world is the consecration of our goodness.

We know it is not the worldly thing to do -- to pray for those who nail us to a cross. But that is just the point: Christianity is not worldliness; it is turning the world upside down. We know it is not "common sense" to love our enemies, for to love our enemies means hating ourselves; but that is the meaning of Christianity -- hating that which is hateful in us. And in reference to Communism let me say: I hate communism because it is destructive of civilization as Russia and Spain so well prove, but *I love the Communists*. I love them because they are the potential children of God.

Our enemy is often our saviour; our persecutor is often our redeemer; our executioners are often our allies, our crucifiers are often our benefactors -- for they reveal what is selfish, base, conceited, and ignoble in us. But we must not hate them for that. To hate them for hating us is weakness.

If we go on answering hate with hate, how will hate ever end? The violent answer to violence is the propagation of further violence; strife increases the sum of bitterness, regardless of who triumphs. Hate is like a seed: if we sow it we reap more hate. If hatred is to be overcome, the sting must be taken out of it; it must not be nourished, or cultivated, or propagated. But how can this be, except by returning good for evil?

How else can we banish hatred from the earth? Suppose 5,000 men are in line and before them is a Communist propagandist telling them that the only way they can overthrow governments and property is by violence, revolution, and the clenched fist. Suppose the first man in line, inspired by that Communist's hatred, strikes the second man in line on the right cheek; the second raises his clenched fist to strike the third; the third wishes to strike the right cheek of the fourth, and on and on clenched fists fly -- because their Gospel is hate.

Is there any way at all to stop that hatred and violence? Yes, on one condition, and that is if one man in that line who is struck on his right cheek, instead of striking his neighbor, turns and offers to the one who struck him his left cheek. He would kill hatred, because he refused to sow it.

Hatred would no longer have soil on which it could grow, for hatred can grow on a right cheek but never on a left cheek: "If any man strikes thee on the right cheek, turn the other cheek."

That is not weakness; it is strength, the strength that makes man master of himself and the conqueror of hate.

If you doubt it, try it sometime to see how much strength it takes. It took so much strength that only Divinity's cry of forgiveness could overcome the hatred of those who crucify.

If you have enemies, if they hate you, if they revile you, and persecute you and say all manner of evil things against you, and you wish to stop their hatred, to release the hatred in their clenched fists, drive them off the face of the earth -- then there is but one way to do it -- *Love them!*

The Cross And The Beatitudes, 1937

Fifth Meditation

Unjust Suffering

"Father, forgive them, for they know not what they do."

The world is full of those who suffer unjustly and who through no fault of their own bear the "slings and arrows of outrageous fortune." What should be our attitude to those who speak untruly of us, who malign our good names, who steal our reputations, and who sneer at our acts of kindness?

The answer is to be found in the first word from the Cross: *forgive*. If there was ever anyone who had a right to protest against injustice it was He Who is Divine Justice; if ever there was anyone who was entitled to reproach those who dug His hands and feet with steel, it was Our Lord on the Cross.

And yet, at that very moment when a tree turns against Him and becomes a cross, when iron turns against Him and becomes nails, when roses turn against Him and become thorns, when men turn against Him and become executioners, He lets fall from His lips for the first time in the history of the world a prayer for enemies: "Father, forgive them, for they know not what they do" *(Luke 23:34)*.

Dwell for a moment on what He did not say. He did not say: "I am innocent," and yet who else could have better claimed innocence? Many times before this Good Friday and many times since, men have been sent to a cross, a guillotine, or a scaffold, for a crime they never committed; but not one of them has ever failed to cry: "I am innocent."

But Our Lord made no such protest, for it would have been to have falsely assumed that man is the Judge of God. Now if Our Lord, Who was Innocence, refrained from asserting His Innocence, then we who are not without sin should not forever be crying our innocence.

To do this is wrongly to admit that man, and not God, is our Judge. Our souls are to be judged not before the tribunal of men, but before the throne of the God of Love; and He "who sees in secret will reward in secret." Our eternal salvation does not depend on how the world judges us, but on how God judges us.

It matters little if our fellow citizens condemn us even when we are right, for Truth always finds its contradictors; that is why Truth is now nailed to a Cross. What does matter is that we be found right in God's judgment, for in that our eternal happiness depends. There is every chance in the world that the two judgments will differ, for man sees only the face, but God reads the heart. We can fool men, but we cannot fool God.

There was another thing Our Blessed Lord did not say to the representatives of Caesar and the Temple who sent Him to the Cross, namely, "You are unjust." The Father gave all judgment unto Him and yet He does not judge man and say: "You will suffer for this." He knew, being God as well as man, that while there is life there is hope, and His patient suffering before death might purchase the souls of many who now condemn.

Why judge them before the time for judgment? Longinus of the Roman army and Joseph of the Sanhedrin would come to His saving embrace and forgiveness even before He was taken down from the Cross. The sinner of this hour might be the saint of the next.

One reason for a long life is penance. Time is given us not just to accumulate that which we cannot take with us, but to make reparation for our sins.

That is why in the parable of the fig tree which had not borne fruit for three years and which the owner wished to cut down because it "cumbereth the ground", the dresser of the vineyard said: "Let it alone this year also, until I dig about it, and dung it. And if happily it bear fruit" *(Luke 13:6-9).*

So the Lord is with the wicked. He gives them another month, another year of life that they may dig their soul with penance and dung it with mortification, and happily save their souls.

If then the Lord did not judge His executioners before the hour of their judgment, why should we, who really know nothing about them anyway, judge them even when they do us wrong? While they live, may not our refraining from judgment be the very means of their conversion? In any case, judgment has not been given to us, and the world may be thankful that it has not, for God is a more merciful judge than man. "Judge not that you may not be judged" *(Matthew 7:1).*

What Our Lord did say on the Cross was, *forgive.* Forgive your Pilates, who are too weak to defend your justice; forgive your Herods, who are too sensual to perceive your spirituality; forgive your Judases, who think worth is to be measured in terms of silver. "Forgive them -- for they know not what they do."

In that sentence is packed the united love of Father and Son, whereby the holy love of God met the sin of man, and remained innocent. This first word of forgiveness is the strongest evidence of Our Lord's absolute sinlessness. The rest of us at our death must witness the great parade of our sins, and the sight of them is so awful that we dare not go before God without a prayer for pardon.

Yet Jesus, on dying, craved no forgiveness, for He had no sin. The forgiveness He asked was for those who accused Him of sin. And the reason He asked for pardon was that "they know not what they do."

He is God as well as man, which means He knows all the secrets of every human heart. Because He knows all, He can find an excuse: "they know not what they do." But we know so little of our enemies' hearts and so little of the circumstances of their acts and the good faith mingled with their evil deeds, that we are less likely to find an excuse. Because we are ignorant of their hearts, we are apt to be less excusing.

In order to judge others, we must be inside them and outside them, but only God can do this. Our neighbors are just as impenetrable to us as we are to them. Judgment on our part, then, would be wrong, for to judge without a mandate is unjust. Our Lord alone has a mandate to judge; we have not.

If possessing that mandate, and knowing all, He still found reason to forgive, then we who have no jurisdiction and who cannot possibly with our puny minds know our neighbors' hearts, have only one thing left to do; that is, to pray: "Father, forgive ... for they know not what they do."

Our Lord used the word, *forgive*, because He was innocent and knew all, but we must use it for other reasons. Firstly, because we have been forgiven greater sins by God. Secondly, because only by forgiving can hate be banished from the world. And thirdly, because our own pardon is conditioned by the pardon we extend to others.

Firstly, we must forgive others because God has forgiven us. There is no injustice any human being has ever committed against us which is comparable to the injustice we commit against God by our sins. It is this idea Our Lord suggests in the parable of the unmerciful servant *(Matthew 18:21-35)* who was forgiven a debt of ten thousand talents by his master, and immediately afterwards went out and choked a fellow-servant who owed him only a hundred pence.

The debt which the master forgave the servant was 1,250,000 times greater than the debt owed by the fellow servant. In this great disproportion is revealed how much greater are man's sins against God than are the sins of our fellowmen against us. We must therefore forgive our enemies, because we have been forgiven the greater sin of treating God as an enemy.

And if we do not forgive the sins of our enemies, it is very likely because we have never cast up our accounts with God. Herein is to be found the secret of so much of the violence and bitterness of some men in our modern world; they refuse to think of themselves as ever having offended God and therefore never think of themselves as needing pardon.

They think they need no pardon, hence no one else should ever have it. The man who knows not his own guilt before God is apt to be most unforgiving to others, as David at the time of his worst sin.

Our condemnation is often the veil for our own weakness: we cover up our own nakedness with the mantle of criticism; we see the mote in our brother's eye, but never the beam in our own. We carry all our neighbor's faults on a sack in front of us, and all our own on a sack behind us.

The cruelest master is the man who never learned to obey, and the severest judge is the man who never examines his own conscience. The man who is conscious of his need of absolution is the one who is most likely to be indulgent to others.

Such was Paul, who, writing to Titus, finds a reason for being merciful to men: "For we ourselves also were some time unwise, incredulous, erring, slaves to divers desires and pleasures, living in malice and envy, hateful, and hating one another" *(Titus 3:3)*.

It is the forgetfulness of its own sins which makes modern hate so deep and bitter. Men throttle their neighbor for a penny because they forget God forgave them a debt of ten thousand talents. Let them only think of how good God has been to them, and they will begin to be good to others.

A second reason for forgiving those who make us suffer unjustly is that if we do not forgive, hate will multiply until the whole world is hateful. Hate is extremely fertile; it reproduces itself with amazing rapidity.

Communism knows hate can disrupt society more quickly than armies, that is why it never speaks of charity. That too is why it sows hatred in labor against capital; hatred in atheists against religion; hatred in themselves against all who oppose them.

How can all this hatred be stopped when one man is slapping another on the cheek? There is only one way, and that is by turning the other cheek, which means: "I forgive; I refuse to hate you. If I hate you, I will add my quota to the sum total of hate. This I refuse to do. I will kill your hate; I will drive it from the earth. I will love you."

That was the way Stephen conquered the hate of those who killed him; namely, by praying: "Lord, lay not this sin to their charge" *(Acts 7:59)*. He was practically repeating the first word from the Cross.

And that prayer of forgiveness won over the heart of a young man named Saul who stood nearby, holding the garments of those who stoned him, and "consenting to his death." If Stephen had cursed Saul, Saul might never have become St. Paul. What a loss that would have been! But hate lost the day because Stephen forgave.

In our day love is still winning victories over hate. When Father Pro of Mexico, a few years ago was shot by the Mexican revolutionists, he turned to them and said: "I forgive you; kneel and I will give you my blessing." And every soldier in the firing line fell on his knees for the blessing.

It was a beautiful spectacle indeed to see a man forgiving those who are about to kill him! Only the Captain refused to kneel, and it was he who did what to Father Pro was an act of great kindness -- ushered him, by a blow through the heart, into the company of Stephen, a martyr of the Church of God.

During the Civil War in Spain when the Reds were slaughtering hundreds of priests, one of them was lined up before the firing squad with his arms tightly bound by ropes. Facing the firing squad, he said: "Untie these ropes and let me give you my blessing before I die." The Communists untied the ropes, but they cut off his hands. Then sarcastically they said: "All right, see if you can give us your blessing now." And the priest raised the stumps of his arms as crimson rags and with blood dripping from them like beads forming on the earth the red rosary of redemption, he moved them about in the form of a cross. Thus hate was defeated, for he refused to nourish it. Hate died as he forgave and the world has been better for it.

Finally, we must forgive others, for on no other condition will our own sins be forgiven. In fact, it is almost a moral impossibility for God to forgive us unless we in turn forgive. Has He not said: "Blessed are the merciful: for they shall obtain mercy" *(Matthew 5:7)*. "Forgive, and you shall be forgiven. Give, and it shall be given unto you . . . For with the same measure that you shall mete withal, it shall be measured to you again" *(Luke 6:37-38)*.

The law is inescapable. Unless we sow, we shall not reap; unless we show mercy to our fellowmen, God will revoke His mercy toward us. As in the parable, the master cancelled the forgiveness of the servant because he refused to show a smaller mercy to his fellowman, "so also shall my heavenly Father do to you, if you forgive not every one, his brother from your hearts" *(Matthew 18:35)*.

If a box is filled with salt it cannot be filled with sand, and if our hearts are filled with hatred of our neighbor, how can God fill them with His love? It is just as simple as that. There can be and there will be no mercy toward us unless we ourselves are merciful. The real test of the Christian then is not how much he loves his friends, but how much he loves his enemies.

The divine command is clear: "Love your enemies: do good to them that hate you: and pray for them that persecute and calumniate you: that you may be the children of your Father who is in heaven, who maketh his sun to rise upon the good, and bad, and raineth upon the just and the unjust.

"For if you love them that love you, what reward shall you have? Do not even the publicans this? And if you salute your brethren only, what do you more? Do not also the heathens this?" *(Matthew 5:44-47).*

Forgive, then! Forgive even seventy times seven! Soften the pillow of death by forgiving your enemies their little sins against you, that you may be forgiven your great sins against God. Forgive those who hate you, that you may conquer them by love. Forgive those who injure you, that you may be forgiven your offenses. Our world is so full of hate!

The race of the clenched fists is multiplying like the race of Cain. The struggle for existence has become existence for struggle. There are even those who talk about peace only because they want the world to wait until they are strong enough for war.

"Dear Lord, what can we, thy followers, do to bring peace to the world? How can we stop brother rising up against brother and class against class, blurring the very sky with their cross-covered Golgothas? Thy First Word on the Cross gives the answer: We must see in the body of every man who hates, a soul that was made to love. If we are too easily offended by their hate, it is because we have forgotten either the destiny of their souls or our own sins. Forgive us our trespasses as we forgive those who trespass against us. Forgive us for ever having been offended. Then we, like Thee, may find among our executioners another Longinus, who had forgotten there was love in a heart until he opened it with a lance."

The Rainbow Of Sorrow, 1938

Sixth Meditation

Anger

"Father, forgive them, for they know not what they do."

The one passion in man that has deeper roots in his rational nature than any other is the passion of anger. Anger and reason are capable of great compatibility, because anger is based upon reason, which weighs the injury done and the satisfaction to be demanded. We are never angry unless someone has injured us in some way -- or we think he has.

But not all anger is sinful, for there is such a thing as just anger. The most perfect expression of just anger we find in Our Blessed Lord's cleansing of the Temple. Passing through its shadowed doorways at the festival of the Pasch, He found greedy traders, victimizing at every turn the worshippers who needed lambs and doves for the temple sacrifices.

Making a scourge of little cords He moved through their midst with a calm dignity and beautiful self-control even more compelling than the whip. The oxen and sheep He drove out with His scourge; with His Hands, He upset the tables of the money changers who scrambled on the floor after their rolling coins; with His finger He pointed to the vendors of doves and bade them leave the outer court; to all He said: "Take these things hence, and make not the house of my Father a house of traffic."

Here was fulfilled the injunction of the Scriptures, "Be angry, and sin not," for anger is no sin under three conditions: 1 -- If the cause of anger be just, for example, defense of God's honor; 2 -- If it is no greater than the cause demands, that is, if it is kept under control; and 3 -- If it is quickly subdued: "Let not the sun go down upon your anger."

Here we are not concerned with just anger, but with unjust anger, namely, that which has no rightful cause -- anger which is excessive, revengeful, and enduring; the kind of anger and hatred against God that has destroyed religion on one sixth of the earth's surface; and which recently in Spain burned 25,000 churches and chapels and murdered 12,000 servants of God: the kind of hatred which is not only directed against God, but also against fellowman, and is fanned by the disciples of class conflict who talk peace but glory in war; the red anger which rushes the blood to the surface, and the white anger which pushes it to the depths and bleaches the face; the anger that seeks to "get even", to repay in kind, bump for bump, punch for punch, eye for eye, lie for lie; the anger of the clenched fist prepared to strike, not in defense of that which is loved but in offense against that which is hated; in a word, the kind of anger that will destroy our civilization unless we smother it by love.

Our Blessed Lord came to make reparation for the sin of anger, first by teaching us a prayer: "Forgive us our trespasses as we forgive those who trespass against us"; and then by giving us a precept: "Love your enemies; do good to them that hate you." More concretely still, He added, "Whosoever will force thee one mile, go with him another two ... if a man ... take away thy coat, let go thy cloak also unto him."

Revenge and retaliation were forbidden: "You have heard that it has been said: an eye for an eye, and a tooth for a tooth. But I say unto you, Love your enemies." These precepts were made all the more striking because He practiced them.

When the Gerasenes became angry at Him because He put a higher value on an afflicted man than on a herd of swine, Scripture records no retort: "And entering into the boat, He passed over the water." To the soldier who struck Him with a mailed fist, He meekly responded: "If I have spoken evil, give testimony of the evil, but if well, why strikest thou me?"

The perfect reparation for anger was made on Calvary. We might also say that anger and hate led Him up that hill. His own people hated Him, for they asked for His crucifixion; the law hated Him, for it forsook justice to condemn Justice; the Gentiles hated Him for they consented to His death; the forests hated Him for one of its trees bore the burden of His weight; the flowers hated Him as they wove thorns for His brow; the bowels of the earth hated Him as it gave its steel as hammer and nails.

Then as if to personalize all that hatred, the first generation of clenched fists in the history of the world stood beneath the Cross and shook them in the face of God. That day they tore His body to shreds as in this day they smash His tabernacle to bits. Their sons and daughters have shattered crucifixes in Spain and Russia as they once smote the Crucified on Calvary.

Let no one think the clenched fist is a phenomenon of the twentieth century; they whose hearts freeze into fists today are but the lineal descendants of those who stood beneath the Cross with hands lifted like clubs against Love as they hoarsely sang the first International of hate.

As one contemplates those clenched fists, one cannot help but feel that if ever anger would have been justified, if ever Justice might have fittingly judged, if ever Power might have rightfully struck, if ever Innocence might have lawfully protested, if ever God might have justly revenged Himself against man -- it was at that moment.

And yet, just at that second when a sickle and a hammer combined to cut down the grass on Calvary's hill to erect a cross, and drive nails through hands to render impotent the blessings of Love incarnate, He, like a tree which bathes in perfume the axe which kills it, let's fall from His lips for the earth's first hearing the perfect reparation for anger and hate -- a prayer for the army of clenched fists, the first Word from the Cross: "Father, forgive them, for they know not what they do."

The greatest sinner may now be saved; the blackest sin may now be blotted out; the clenched fist may now be opened; the unforgivable may now be forgiven. While they were most certain that they knew what they were doing, He seizes upon the only possible palliation of their crime and urges it upon His Heavenly Father with all the ardor of a merciful Heart: ignorance -- "they know not what they do." If they did know what they were doing as they fastened Love to a tree, and still went on doing it, they would never be saved. They would be *damned.*

It is only because fists are clenched in ignorance that they may yet be opened into folded hands; it is only because tongues blaspheme in ignorance that they may yet speak in prayer. It is not their conscious wisdom that saves them; it is their unconscious ignorance.

This Word from the Cross teaches us two lessons: 1 -- The reason for forgiving is ignorance; and 2 -- There are no limits to forgiveness.

The reason for forgiving is ignorance. Divine Innocence found such a reason for pardon; certainly guilt can do no less. St. Peter's first Pentecostal sermon used this very excuse of ignorance for the Crucifixion so fresh in his mind: "The author of life you killed . . . and now, brethren, I know that you did it through ignorance, as did also your rulers."

If there were full consciousness of the evil, perfect deliberation, perfect understanding of the consequences of acts, there would be no room for forgiveness. That is why there is no redemption for the fallen angels. They knew what they were doing. We do not. We are very ignorant -- ignorant of ourselves and ignorant of others.

Ignorant of others! How little we know of their motives, their good faith, the circumstances surrounding their actions. When others visit violence upon us we too often forget how little we know about their hearts and say: "I cannot see that they have the slightest excuse; they knew very well what they were doing." And yet in exactly the same circumstances, Jesus found an excuse: "They know not what they do."

We know nothing about the inside of our neighbor's heart and hence we refuse to forgive. He knew the heart inside out, and because He did know, He forgave. Take any scene of action, let five people look upon it, and you will get five different stories of what happened. No one of them sees all sides. Our Lord does, and that is why He forgives.

Why is it that we can find excuses for our anger against our neighbor, and yet we refuse to admit the same excuses when our neighbor is angry with us? We say others would forgive us if they understood us perfectly, and that the only reason they are angry with us is because "they do not understand."

Why is not that ignorance reversible? Can we not be as ignorant of their motives, as we say they are ignorant of ours? Does not our refusal to find an excuse for their hatred tacitly mean that under similar circumstances, we ourselves will be unfit to be forgiven?

Ignorance of ourselves is another reason for forgiving others. Unfortunately, it is ourselves we know least; our neighbor's sins, weaknesses and failures we know a thousand times better than our own. Criticism of others may be bad, but it is want of self-criticism, which is worse.

It would be less wrong to criticize others if we first criticized ourselves, for if we first turned the searchlight into our own souls, we would never feel we had a right to turn it on the soul of anyone else. It is only because we are ignorant of our true condition that we fail to realize how badly we stand in need of pardon.

Have we ever offended God? Has He any right to be angry with us? Then why should we, who need pardon so badly, strive not to purchase it by pardoning others? The answer is because we never examine our own consciences.

We are so ignorant of our true condition that we know little more of ourselves than our name and address and how much we have; of our selfishness, our envy, our detraction, our sin, we know absolutely nothing. In fact, in order that we may never know ourselves, we hate silence and solitariness. Lest our conscience should carry on with us an unbearable repartee, we drown out its voice in amusements, distractions, and noise. If we met ourselves in others, we would hate them.

If we knew ourselves better, we would be more forgiving of others. The harder we are on ourselves, the easier we will be on others; the man who has never learned to obey knows not how to command; and the man who has never disciplined himself knows not how to be merciful.

It is always the selfish who are unkind to others, and those who are hardest on themselves are the kindest to others, as the teacher who knows the least is always the most intolerant to his pupils.

Only a Lord who thought so little of Himself as to become man and die like a criminal could ever forgive the weakness of those who crucified Him.

It is not hatred that is wrong; it is hating the wrong thing that is wrong. It is not anger that is wrong, it is being angry at the wrong thing that is wrong. Tell me your enemy, and I will tell you what you are. Tell me your hatred, and I will tell you your character.

Do you hate religion? Then your conscience bothers you. Do you hate the capitalists? Then you are avaricious, and you want to be a capitalist. Do you hate the laborer? Then you are selfish and a snob. Do you hate sin? Then you love God. Do you hate your hate, your selfishness, your quick temper, and your wickedness? Then you are a good soul, for "If any man come to me . . . and hate not his own life, he cannot be my disciple."

The second lesson to be derived from this First Word from the Cross is that there is no limit to pardon. Our Lord forgave when He was innocent and not because He Himself had been forgiven. Hence we must forgive not only when we have been forgiven, but even when we are innocent.

The problem of the limits of pardon once troubled Peter, and He asked our Lord: "How often shall my brother offend against me, and I forgive him till seven times?" Peter thought he was stretching forgiveness by saying "seven times," for it was four more than the Jewish Masters enjoined.

Peter proposed a limit beyond which there was to be no forgiveness. Peter assumed the right to be forgiven is automatically renounced after seven offenses. It is equivalent to saying, "I renounce my right to collect debts from you if you never owe me more than seven dollars, but if you exceed that sum, then my duty of further cancellation ceases. I can throttle you for eight dollars."

Our Lord, in answering Peter says that forgiveness has no limits; forgiveness is the surrender of all rights and the denial of limits. "I say not to thee till seven times but till seventy times seven." That does not mean 490 literally, but infinitely. The Saviour then proceeded to tell the parable of the unjust steward who immediately after being forgiven by his lord a debt of 10,000 talents, choked a fellow servant who owed him a hundred pence. The unmerciful steward by refusing to be merciful to his debtor had his own mercy revoked. His guilt was not that, needing mercy he refused to show it, but having received mercy, he was unmerciful still. "So also shall my heavenly Father do to you if you forgive not every one his brother."

Forgive then, and we will be forgiven; remit our anger against others and God will remit His anger against us. Judgment is a harvest where we sow what we reap. If we sowed anger against our brethren during life, we will reap the just anger of God. Judge not, and we shall not be judged.

If, during life, we forgive others from our hearts, on Judgment Day the All Wise God will permit something very unusual to Himself: He will forget how to add and will know only how to subtract. He who has a memory from all eternity will no longer remember our sins. Thus, we will be saved once again through Divine "Ignorance."

By forgiving others on the ground that they know not what they do, Our Lord will forgive us on the ground that He no longer remembers what we did. It may well be that if He looks on a hand that, now after hearing the first Word on the Cross gives a kindly blessing to an enemy, He will even forget that it was once a clenched fist red with the blood of Christendom.

"And dars't thou venture still to live in sin,
And crucify thy dying Lord again?
Were not His pangs sufficient? Must he bleed
Yet more? O, must our sinful pleasures feed
Upon his torments, and augment the story
Of the sad passion of the Lord of glory!
Is there no pity? Is there no remorse
In human breasts? Is there a firm divorce
Betwixt all mercy and the hearts of men?
Parted forever – ne'er to meet again?
No Mercy bides with us: 'tis thou alone,
Hast it, sweet Jesu, for us, that have none
For thee: thou hast forestall'd our markets so
That all's above, and we have none below:
Nay, blessed Lord, we have not wherewithal
To serve our shiftless selves: unless we call
To thee, thou art our Saviour, and hast power
To give, and whom we crucify each hour:
We are cruel, Lord, to thee and ourselves too;
Jesu forgive us; we know not what we do."

(Francis Quarles)

Victory Over Vice, 1939

Seventh Meditation

Fortitude

"Father, forgive them, for they know not what they do."

There is entirely too much psycho-analysis in the world; what is needed is a little more psycho-synthesis. Hearts and minds have been analyzed to a point where they are nothing more than a chaotic mass of unrelated nerve impulses. There is need for someone to pull them together, to give them a pattern of life and above all, peace. The pattern around which we shall psycho-synthesize all these soul-states will be the Cross.

Here we are interested in three types of souls: a) Those who suffer and mourn, saying "What have I done to deserve this?"; b) those who possess faith, but who through a love of the world deny their faith or hide it; c) and those who do not possess the faith, but are convinced of its truth and yet refuse to pay the price.

There is a virtue, which these three types of souls need for their peace, and that is the virtue of Fortitude.

Fortitude may be defined as that virtue which enables us to face undismayed and fearlessly the difficulties and dangers which stand in the way of duty and goodness. It stands midway between foolhardiness, which rushes into danger heedlessly, and cowardice, which flees from it recreantly. Because fortitude is related to bravery, it must not be thought that bravery is devoid of fear; rather it is control of fear. Fortitude is of two kinds, depending upon whether it is directed to a natural good or a supernatural good.

A soldier, for example, who braves the dangers of battle for love of country practices natural fortitude. But the saint who overcomes all difficulties and dangers for the sake of the glory of God and the salvation of his soul, practices supernatural fortitude.

It is in the presence of the fear of death that Fortitude reaches its peak; that is why the highest peak of supernatural fortitude is martyrdom. We are here concerned only with supernatural fortitude.

This virtue reaches its peak in practice in the life of Our Divine Lord: He was primarily a Redeemer -- God in the form of man saving men of whom He was King and Captain. "For God sent not his Son into the world, to judge the world, but that the world may be saved by him" *(John 3:17).*

His baptism was death and He was "straitened until it be accomplished" *(Luke 12:50).* Being truly a man, He felt the fear every normal man feels in the face of danger. "If it be possible, let this chalice pass from Me" *(Matthew 26:39)*; but resigned to the Father's business, He added: "Nevertheless not as I will, but as thou wilt" *(Matthew 26:39).*

No difficulty, however great, would deter Him from the Divine purpose of laying down His life for the redemption of many. Not even "twelve legions of Angels" *(Matthew 26:53)* would He permit to solace Him in His darkest hour, and not even a drug would He touch to His lips to deaden the pains of the Cross.

Solomon of old had said: "Give strong drink to them that are sad, and wine to them that are grieved in mind: Let them drink and forget their want, and remember their sorrow no more" *(Proverbs 31:6,7).*

The Talmud says it was the custom to put a grain of incense in the draft of those who were being led to death, to deaden the sense of pain.

This intoxicating draft which was given Him as His hands and feet were nailed to a tree of His own creation, He refused to drink *(Matthew 27:34).*

He strides forth boldly to the high things of God. He will meet death in the full possession of His faculties -- fearlessly.

But not in this was His fortitude greatest: when death is upon Him by His own submission, for "no man taketh it away from me: but I lay it down of myself" *(John 10:18)*, His first word from the Cross is not in self-defence, not a protestation of His own innocence, not a fear of death nor a plea for deliverance, nor even fear of enemies.

Fear of death makes most men turn away from doing good. It makes even innocent men thoughtful of themselves as they proclaim their innocence to their executioners. Not so with Him. Fortitude reaches the peak of self-forgetfulness. On the Cross He thinks only of others and their salvation.

For His first word is not about death, but about the good it will accomplish; it is directed not to His friends, His Apostles, or His believers who will proclaim His gospel, but to those who hate Him and His Apostles and His Church: "Father, forgive them, for they know not what they do" *(Luke 23:34)*.

Often during His life, He preached: "Love your enemies: do good to them that hate you" *(Matthew 5:44)*. Now that He is strong enough to ignore death, He the Conqueror bestows on His momentary conquerors the very thing they had forfeited by their sins -- forgiveness.

Why is it that He appeals to His Father to forgive, and does not Himself forgive directly? Because He is looking at the crucifixion not from the human point of view, but from the Divine. They were wronging the Father by killing His Divine Son. The crucifixion is not murder; it is *deicide*.

Murder is a sin against God Who gave human life to human care. Deicide is a sin against God Who entrusted Divine Life to human love. It was not the candle of a man's life the executioners were snuffing out; it was the sun they were trying to extinguish.

The noon-day sun never darkened on murder, but it hid its face in shame as the Light of the World went into the momentary eclipse of death.

No stronger proclamation of His Divinity could have been uttered than for the Divine Son to ask the Divine Father to forgive the sons of men for their Golgothas, their swastikas, and their hammers and sickles. If He were only a man He would have asked His own forgiveness, but being God He asked His Father for the pardon of men.

Scripture does not record that anyone except the Thief on the right, within the hearing of that cry, repented or even regretted driving the nails and unfurling the flag of the Cross to the four winds of the world. There is not a single record that anyone else expressed a desire to follow Him or that they were touched by His calmness under fire.

Thus the world's greatest act of bravery when He who was thoughtless of self became thoughtful of others, went momentarily barren. They were apparently satisfied to sit and watch.

But it was for a bigger world than Calvary that He died, and for greater harvests than Jerusalem that He suffered. "And not for them only do I pray, but for them also who through their word shall believe in me" *(John 17:20).*

Now that the Divine Physician has prepared the medicine, apply it to the first of our three types of souls, namely, those who suffer and mourn saying: "What have I done to deserve this? "

There are many good men and women tossing on beds of pain, their bodies wasted by long sickness, their hearts broken with woe and sorrow, or their minds tortured by irreparable loss of friends and fortune. If these souls want peace they must recognize that in this world there is no intrinsic connection between personal sin and suffering.

One day "Jesus passing by, saw a man, who was blind from his birth: And his disciples asked him: Rabbi, who hath sinned, this man, or his parents, that he should be born blind? Jesus answered: Neither hath this man sinned, nor his parents" *(John 9:1-3)*.

That brings us face to face with the inscrutable will of God which we cannot understand, any more than a mouse in a piano can understand why a musician disturbs him by playing. Our puny minds cannot understand the mysteries of God. But there are two basic truths which such burdened souls must never surrender, otherwise they will never find peace. First, God is love.

Hence anything He does to me deserves my gratitude and I will say "thank you." God is still good even though He does not give me whatever I *want* in this world. He gives me only what I *need* for the next.

Parents do not give five-year-old boys guns to play with, though there is hardly a boy of five who does not want a gun. As Job put it: "If we have received good things at the hand of God, why should we not receive evil?" *(Job 2:10)*.

Second, the final reward for virtue comes not in this life, but in the next. As tapestries are woven not from the front but from the back, so too in this life we see only the underside of God's plan.

"My life is but a weaving
Between my God and me.
I may but choose the colors
He worketh skilfully.

Full oft He chooses sorrow,
And I, in foolish pride,
Forget He sees the upper,
And I the under, side."

    (Father Tabb)

We are not to have our moods made by the world; the world should revolve about us; not us about the world. Like the earth in its revolution about the sun we will carry our own atmosphere with us -- resignation to the will of God. Then nothing can ever happen against our will, because our will is the will of God.

This is not fatalism, which is subjection to blind necessity; it is patience, which is resignation to the will of the Divine Love who in the end can desire nothing but the eternal happiness and perfection of the one loved.

Fatalism is nonsense as the man walking precariously on the railing of a ship in a stormy sea proved when he said to the worried onlookers: "I'm a fatalist."

But patient resignation is exemplified by the child who said to her father: "Daddy, I do not know why you want me to go to the hospital for that operation. It hurts. I know only that you love me."

The shock of sorrow comes only to those who think this world is fixed and absolute, that there is nothing beyond. They think everything here below should be perfect. Hence they ask questions: "Why should I suffer? What have I done to deserve this?" Maybe you did nothing to deserve it. Certainly Our Lord did nothing to deserve His Cross. But it came and through it He went to His glory.

The virtue to be cultivated then by such souls is what is known as Patience. Patience and Fortitude are related as the convex and concave sides of a saucer. Fortitude is exercised in the active struggle with dangers and difficulties, while Patience is the passive acceptance of what is hard to bear.

Our Lord on the Cross practiced Fortitude by freely and fearlessly meeting death to purchase our forgiveness; He practiced Patience by passively accepting the Father's will.

Being God, He could have stepped down from the Cross. Twelve legions of angels could have ministered to His wounds, the earth could have been His footstool, the seas as healing balm, the sun as His chariot, the planets His cortège, and the Cross His triumphal throne. But He willed to accept death to give us an example: "Not my will, but thine be done" *(Luke 22:42)*.

Passive acceptance of God's will is Patience. Patience, other things being equal, is nobler than Fortitude; for in active works we may choose what pleases us and thereby sometimes deceive ourselves, but in resignation to the crosses of life it is always God's will that we do.

"In your patience," He said, "you shall possess your souls" *(Luke 21:19)*. In His Patience, He possesses His, for He did not choose His Cross, it was made for Him. He was fitted and patterned to it; we might almost say cut to fit it.

To take the Cross God sends us as He took the one given to Him, even though we do not deserve it, is the shortest way to identification with God's will which is the beginning of Power and Peace: Power because we are one with Him who can do all things; Peace because we are tranquil in the love of Him who is just.

Dare we call ourselves Christian and expect another road to heaven than that which Christ Himself travelled? Love leads the way -- it is enough for us to follow the Beloved knowing that He loves and cares. Then instead of seeking to have a road free of obstacles to attain God, we shall, like hurdles in the race of life, make a race out of obstacles.

Embracing the crosses of life because given to us by Love on the Cross, does not mean that any of us ever reach the stage where our nature is willing to suffer. On the contrary our nature rebels against it, because it is contrary to nature. But we can will *supernaturally* what nature rejects, just as our reason can accept what the senses reject.

My eyes tell me I should not let the doctor lance the festering boil, for it will hurt. But my reason tells me that my senses must momentarily submit to the pain for the sake of a future good. So too we can will to bear the unavoidable ills of life for *supernatural* reasons. The First Word from the Cross suggests doing so for the sake of the *remission* of sins: "Forgive them."

In the business world, we contract debts and recognize our obligation and duty to acquit them. Why should we think that in the same moral universe we can sin with impunity? If then we bear the imprints of the Cross, instead of complaining against God let us occasionally think of offering them up to God for our own sins, or for the sins of our neighbors.

Of all the nonsense our modern world has invented, nothing surpasses the catchwords or claptrap we give the unfortunate or the sick: "Keep your chin up" or "Forget it." This is not solace, but a drug. Consolation is in explaining suffering, not forgetting it; in relating it to Love, not ignoring it; in making it an expiation for sin, not another sin. But who shall understand this unless he looks at a Cross and loves the Crucified?

The second type of soul who can be helped by this First Word from the Cross is he who, possessing the great gift of Faith, out of love of the world either hides it or denies it. This applies to those lukewarm Catholics who say: "Of course I ate meat at the party on Friday. Did you think I was going to have everyone laughing at me?" "Yes, I sent my son to a non-Catholic college. They are more social you know, and I don't want my boy to meet policemen's sons." Or, "When that chap at the office ridiculed the Mass, I did not say I was a Catholic, for the boss is anti-Catholic and I might lose my job."

Doubtlessly such spineless Catholics would fit the spirit of the world better if they gave up their faith. Business men could then meet the challenge of chiseling competitors; the passion of youth could have its fling; husbands could have second wives; wives could have third husbands; both husbands and wives could find an alternative to self-restraint and thus escape the comparative poverty attendant upon raising a family; politicians could improve their chances for election if they were less Catholic; lawyers could be richer if they did not have to confess their sins and make amends; doctors could be wealthier if they were less conscientious and ceased to believe in Divine Justice.

There is no challenging the fact that Catholics could get on better with the world if they were less Catholic.

Not a single sentence can be found in the words of our Divine Lord promising you the love of the world because of your faith. But you can find a golden string of texts warning you that the world will hate you because you are His: "If you had been of the world, the world would love its own: but because you are not of the world, but I have chosen you out of the world, therefore the world hateth you" *(John 15:19).*

"Every one therefore that shall confess me before men, I will also confess him before my Father who is in heaven. But he that shall deny me before men, I will also deny him before my Father who is in heaven . . . And he that taketh not up his cross, and followeth me, is not worthy of me. He that findeth his life, shall lose it and he that shall lose his life for me, shall find it" *(Matthew 10:32-33, 38-39).*

"How narrow is the gate, and strait is the way that leadeth to life: and few there are that find it" *(Matthew 7:14).*

"For he that shall be ashamed of me, and of my words, in this adulterous and sinful generation: the Son of man also will be ashamed of him, when he shall come in the glory of his Father with the holy angels" *(Mark 8:38; Cf. Luke 9:26).*

"If we suffer, we shall also reign with him. If we deny him, he will also deny us" *(2Timothy 2:12).*

"And if thy right hand scandalize thee, cut it off, and cast it from thee: for it is expedient for thee that one of thy members should perish, rather than that thy whole body go into hell" *(Matthew 5:30)*.

The true followers of Christ were meant to be at odds with the world: The pure of heart will be laughed at by the Freudians; the meek will be scorned by the Marxists; the humble will be walked on by the go-getters; the liberal Sadducees will call them reactionaries; the reactionary Pharisees will call them liberals.

And Our Lord so warned: "Blessed are ye when they shall revile you, and persecute you, and speak all that is evil against you, untruly, for my sake: Be glad and rejoice for your reward is very great in heaven. For so they persecuted the prophets that were before you" *(Matthew 5:11)*.

To all those compromising Catholics, a plea is made to practice the Fortitude of the Saviour on the Cross who, being thoughtless of death for the sake of our forgiveness, taught us to be thoughtless of the world's scorn for the sake of being forgiven.

We must not forget the word of Our Saviour: "He that shall deny me before men, I will also deny him before my Father who is in heaven" *(Matthew 10:33)*. And if Catholics will not be strong in their love of Christ because of Christ, then let them be strong out of fear of the scandal of their weakness.

The example of a bad Catholic is most often appealed to as a justification for evil. Why is it that the world is more scandalized at a bad Catholic than a bad anything else, if it be not because his fall is rightfully measured by the heights from which he has fallen.

And let this fortitude be not a muscular fortitude, or abusive fortitude, but a fortitude brave enough to declare the belief in God even among the enemies who nail us to the cross of scorn, a fortitude like unto that of Eleazar, who, when commanded by Antiochus the enemy of the Jews to eat forbidden meat and who was advised by his own friends to do so, answered: "It doth not become our age . . . to dissemble . . . Though, for the present time, I should be delivered from the punishments of men, yet should I not escape the hand of the Almighty neither alive nor dead" (2Maccabees 6:24, 26).

The third type of soul to whom this First Word offers Fortitude comprises those who are convinced of the truth of the faith but are unwilling to pay the price. A price does have to be paid for conversion, and that price is scorn. Many souls stand poised between an inner conviction that the Church is true and the certitude that if they embrace it they must make enemies.

Once they cross its threshold a thinly veiled hostility often takes the place of friendship. They may be accused of having lost their reason; their jobs may be endangered; their friends who believed in freedom of conscience may now turn against them because their consciences acted freely; their love of liturgy will be scorned, as superstition and their supernatural faith will be called credulity.

If they joined a crazy cult or became a sun worshipper or a Yogi follower or founded a new religion, their friends would say they acted within their constitutional rights; but when they join the Church, some will say they lost their minds, as they told Our Lord He had a devil.

Why this revolution of attitude once the threshold of the Church has been passed? Very simply because entering into the Church lifts us into another world -- the supernatural world. It gives us a new set of values, a new objective, new ways of thinking, new standards of judgment, all of which are in opposition to the spirit of the world.

The world with its hatred of discipline, its courtesy to the flesh, and its indifference to truth, cannot tolerate a life based upon the primacy of Christ and the salvation of souls. "I have chosen you out of the world, therefore the world hateth you. If you had been of the world, the world would love its own . . . [but] know ye, that it hath hated me before you" (John 15:19, 18).

Most people today want a religion which suits the way they live, rather than one which makes demands upon them. The result is that in order to make religion popular, too many prophets have watered down religion until it is hardly distinct from sentimental secularism. Religion thus becomes a luxury like an opera, not a responsibility like life.

There is no doubt that a religion which makes concessions to human weakness will be popular; for example, one that denies hell for those who are unjust, and is silent about divorce for those who have repudiated their vows.

But as Catholics, we may not tamper with the message of Christ; for religion is of His making not ours. Furthermore, the only religion which will help the world is one which contradicts the world.

Most Americans have been so disillusioned by a Cross-less Christ, that they are now looking back to the Cross as the only point of reference which gives meaning to life. They may not know how to phrase the conflict within, but they dimly perceive that all unhappiness is due to a conflict of wills: Family quarrels arise that way; misery of souls arises that way too when our selfish will contradicts the Divine will.

Peace, we are just discovering, is in the identity of our will with God who wills our perfection. When we disobey His will we are not asserting our independence; we are mutilating our personality as we might mutilate a razor by using it to cut a tree. Being made for God, we can be happy only with Him.

All our misery is traceable to that rebellion. All our peace is traceable to training the lower part of ourselves in service to Him. Hence the Cross, the symbol of that sacrifice inspired by love.

The Seven Virtues, 1940

Eighth Meditation

A Word To Humanists

There are millions of souls in this great country of ours who have no religion whatsoever. Their attitudes vary from an earnest yearning for religion to an intense hatred of it. It is quite possible that all of them could be reduced to seven distinct categories.

Our Lord spoke seven times *from* the Cross -- and these are called His Seven Last Words. But those who were on Calvary's Hill that afternoon addressed seven words to Him on the Cross, thus revealing the seven different impacts the Cross makes on souls.

The seven words, which Our Lord spoke *from* the Cross were not specific answers to specific challenges, but they do reveal lessons applicable to the challenge.

The first of seven possible attitudes toward the Cross is that of Humanism, for the first group to challenge the Cross was the Humanists. The term Humanist is here understood in the modern philosophical sense, and embraces all those who want a religion without a Cross. They believe that man is naturally good, that progress is inevitable through science, and that human reason by its own effort is able to restore peace to the world and to consciences.

They regard all suggestions about faith, grace, and the supernatural order as impractical and unnecessary. They want an education of self-expression, a God without justice, a morality without religion, a Christ without a Cross, a Christianity without sacrifice, a Kingdom of God without redemption.

These Humanists of our day had their prototypes on Calvary on Good Friday. They were those whom Sacred Scripture calls the "passers-by"; a significant term indeed for it suggests those who never remain long enough with religion to know anything about it, those who think themselves wise because they have had a passing acquaintance with Christ.

It is they who speak the First Word to the Cross: "Vah, thou that destroyest the temple of God, and in three days dost rebuild it; save thy own self: if thou be the Son of God, come down from the Cross" *(Matthew 27:40)*.

He is no sooner on the Cross than they ask Him *to* come down. "Come down from your belief in divinity! Come down from your teaching of hell! Come down from your belief that what God hath joined together no man may put asunder! Come down from your belief that Christ will preserve Peter from the gates of hell even to the consummation of the world! Come down from your belief in infallibility! Come down and we will believe!"

And while the mob jeers, there comes from the Cross the answer: "Father, forgive them, for they know not what they do." They said: "*If* thou be the Son of God." Humanists are certain only of humanity, not of divinity.

But He spoke of God: "Father." they said: "Come down." They judged power by deliverance from pain. He said: "Forgive." He judged power by deliverance from sin. They boasted of their knowledge and superior wisdom, and He reminded them that all their wisdom was ignorance: "They know not what they do."

Religion, the Humanists insist, must be love! And who speaks more of brotherhood than humanists? But they want Love without a Cross. And that Our Blessed Lord seems to imply is impossible, for how shall love forgive without first satisfying justice? Shall love mean, "to let the sinner go on sinning" or shall it mean "to make the sinner sinless"?

A religion without a Cross! That is the essence of Humanism. What we want to do here is not to prove the Humanists wrong, but to try to make them understand the meaning of the Cross and how much it symbolizes the love to God. I speak directly to them.

Humanists: You have humanized God, and thus you have dehumanized man. By denying man is supernatural you have not left him even *natural*. For every man wants to be more than he is.

You have tried to make all men brothers, but have you not forgotten that men cannot be brothers unless they have a common Father, and God cannot be a Father unless He has a Son -- to whom we all are patterned as brothers?

Swine are content. But you Humanists are not content with humanity, wherein, like monsters of the deep, man preys on man!

You want humanity to be humane. But if there be no model for humaneness, how shall men be modeled?

Look to your doctrines of man: Whence came that which is best in him, if it be not from the Best and Holiest?

In Godless hands man has withered like a rose without roots.

You make indeed a Republic of Kings, but you have no one to crown or anoint them.

The tragedy of your Humanism is believing that dirty things are clean, that cruel are kind, that hence there is no need of a Cross: "Come down and we will believe." To you, all men are good. There are halos even in hell.

And so on Calvary's Hill you stand and ask in wisdom for a Christ without a Cross, while He answers: "Forgive!"

Do you not know that to have a world without a Cross is in itself a cross? Do you know a mother worthy of the name who would not, out of love, take the pain of her tender babe as her very own, because she loves? Why then should not Supreme Love, in the face of evil, seek to take the penalty which sin deserves, that the evil might be innocent again?

Then why do you say: "Come down and we will believe"? If He came down, in whom would you believe?

Humanists, why are we at war if it be not because sin is in some human blood, and only in the shedding of just blood can there be remission of that sin?

Why not see then that great evils can be conquered only by a God-made-man upon a Cross? Why do you say: "Come down and we will believe"? For if He came down where would love be? "Greater love than this no man hath, that a man lay down his life for his friends" *(John 15:13)*.

To avoid a war, when it alone can preserve justice, is not sanctity, you say, but vile surrender! Then to avoid a Cross which alone can redeem from sin, is not human. It is ignorance of man's great needs.

He that made your eye, shall He not see? He that made your ear, shall He not hear? He that made your soldiers, brave enough to die, may not He Himself be a Captain dying to make wrong right?

Then why do you say: "Come down and we will believe"? Do you believe that you, who out of love of neighbor can sacrifice yourself, can do that which God cannot do? Truly! You know not what you do.

Have you Humanists ever seen Love stand up against brute Force and go down because it would not cease to love? If then you bless the Sermon on the Mount, wherein love was preached, why do you curse the Sermon on the Cross, where Love met hate and died? Is not Calvary inseparable from the Mount, for love preached to evil must be crucified.

Love without Power is destroyed by evil. But Love armed with power will die rather than surrender goodness.

God must suffer too as man suffers. Else how can Love be love if it costs not the Lover? Did not your Goethe say: "If I were God this world of sin would break my heart"? Well, that is just what it did to Christ! It broke His Heart!

Why then, if your love for man is sometimes met by sneer and scorn, do you say to a Christ whose God-love was crucified: "Come down and we will believe"? In what can you believe, if Love must love without a Cross?

Not from any talisman of ancient times, but from heaven itself, has come the Cross. For there is "the Lamb, which was slain from the beginning of the world" *(Revelation 13:8)*. From that primal day when the shedding of a brother's blood cried up to the heavens, to this very hour when the race of Abel lies slain by the jealous brethren of the race of Cain, the spilling of unjust blood cries out to heaven, until God heard, and came down as man to shed His blood, that a man might be more than a man -- Aye! A very child of God!

The Cross is eternal! It cannot be dug up; it cannot be taken down! It is the core of creation! It is the root of all our lesser Calvaries! Then why do you say: "Come down and we will believe"?

It is God who gives us the Cross. And it is the Cross that gives us God.

You want the Cross but not the crucifix. The cross you wear can be a charm, but the crucifix cannot. Somehow, when you see it, you feel involved! A statue of Buddha does not stir you. Put a crucifix on your desk for three days, and see what it does to you!

Humanists! Remember the days of the French revolution, when a mob swept into the Tuilleries, through room after room it went, destroying. Then, through a closed door, and, lo and behold: a chapel! Above the tabernacle hung the crucifix. A hush fell upon the enraged mob.

Someone cried: "Hats off." Every head was bowed, then every knee was bent. Indifference was impossible. Then a humanist took the crucifix down, hung it in an adjoining house, and the wild tide of destruction rolled on! They had taken the Christ down from the Cross! Now they could proceed! Religion now was comfortable!

No wonder men want Christ to come down! They want a Cross but not a crucifix. A crucifix perils your soul. You stand unmoved before the Sphinx -- but the Christ on His Cross involves you in Its guilt.

Suppose the Christ upon that Cross came down as you bade! He would have forced you then to do His will; and where then would be your freedom? One day He will come without His Cross! Bearing it rather than being borne! But that will be to judge and strike and not to heal, as now; for then the time of healing will be past!

The human never long remains the Humanist, for either beast or angel he becomes, but not just man! If you came from the beast you cannot leave the beast behind. But if you came from God then you can leave humanity behind and be a child of God! This is true Humanism, where man finds his center in his Source.

Before 'tis too late, dear Humanists, desist your plea: "Come down and we will believe." But harken: "Father! Forgive." Forgiveness is not cheap. If He offered it without a Cross, you would not take it. But from a nail-pierced hand, how could you refuse? That Cross is the price God paid to buy you from your sins. Without it, there is neither sin nor God.

As you rise in the scale of nobility, do you not choose pain and trouble rather than comfort and ease? Then why not choose Him who did just that for you?

Seven Words To The Cross, 1944

Ninth Meditation

The Value of Ignorance

One thousand years before Our Blessed Lord was born, there lived one of the greatest of all poets: the glorious Homer of the Greeks. Two great epics are ascribed to him: one the Iliad; the other, the Odyssey. The hero of the Iliad was not Achilles, but Hector, the leader of the enemy Trojans whom Achilles defeated and killed. The poem ends not with the glorification of Achilles but of the defeated Hector.

The other poem, the Odyssey, has as its hero, not Odysseus, but Penelope, his wife, who was faithful to him during the years of his travels. As the suitors pressed for her affections, she told them that when she finished weaving the garment they saw before her, she would listen to their courtship. But each night she unraveled what she had woven in the day, and thus remained faithful until her husband returned. "Of all women," she said, "I am the most sorrowful." Well might be applied to her the words of Shakespeare: "Sorrow sits in my soul as on a throne. Bid kings come and bow down to it."

For a thousand years before the birth of Our Blessed Lord, pagan antiquity resounded with these two stories of the poet who threw into the teeth of history the mysterious challenge of glorifying a defeated man and hailing a sorrowful woman. How, the subsequent centuries asked, could anyone be victorious in defeat and glorious in sorrow? And the answer was never given until that day when there came One Who was glorious in defeat: the Christ on His Cross and one who was magnificent in sorrow: His Blessed Mother beneath the cross.

It is interesting that Our Lord spoke seven times on Calvary and that His Mother is recorded as having spoken but seven times in Sacred Scripture. Her last recorded word was at the Marriage Feast of Cana, when her Divine Son began His Public Life. Now that the sun was out, there was no longer need of the moon to shine. Now that the Word has spoken, there was no longer need of words.

St. Luke records five of the seven words which he could have known only from her. St. John records the other two. One wonders, as Our Blessed Lord spoke each of His Seven Words, if Our Blessed Mother at the foot of the Cross did not think of each of her corresponding words. Such will be the subject of our meditation: Our Lord's Seven Words on the Cross and the Seven Words of Mary's Life.

Men cannot stand weakness. Men are, in a certain sense, the weaker sex. There is nothing that so much unnerves a man as a woman's tears. Therefore men need the strength and the inspiration of women who do not break down in a crisis. They need someone not prostrate at the foot of the cross, but standing, as Mary stood. John was there; he saw her standing, and he wrote it down in his Gospel.

Generally, when innocent men suffer at the hands of impious judges, their last words are either: "I am innocent" or "The courts are rotten." But here, for the first time in the hearing of the world, is one who asked neither for the forgiveness of His own sins, for He is God, nor proclaimed His own innocence, for men are not judges of God. Rather does He plead for those who kill him: "Father, forgive them, for they know not what they do" *(Luke 23:34).*

Mary beneath the gibbet heard Her Divine Son speak that First Word. I wonder when she heard him say, "know not" if she did not recall her own First Word. It, too, contained those words: "know not."

The occasion was the Annunciation, the first good news to reach the earth in centuries. The angel announced to her that she was to become the Mother of God: "Behold thou shalt conceive in thy womb and shalt bring forth a son: and thou shalt call his name Jesus. He shall be great and shall be called the son of the Most High. And the Lord God shall give unto him the throne of David his father: and he shall reign in the house of Jacob forever. And of his Kingdom there shall be no end. And Mary said to the Angel: How shall this be done, because I know not man?" *(Luke 1:31-34).*

These words of Jesus and Mary seem to suggest that there is sometimes wisdom in not knowing. Ignorance is here represented not as a cure, but a blessing. This rather shocks our modern sensibilities which so much glorify education, but that is because we fail to distinguish between true wisdom and false wisdom. St. Paul called the wisdom of the world "foolishness," and Our Blessed Lord thanked His Heavenly Father that He had not revealed Heavenly Wisdom to the worldly wise.

The ignorance which is here extolled is not ignorance of the truth, but ignorance of evil. Notice it first of all in the word of Our Saviour to His executioners: He implied that they could be forgiven only because they were ignorant of their terrible crime. It was not their wisdom that would save them, but their ignorance.

If they knew what they were doing as they smote the Hands of Everlasting Mercy, dug the Feet of the Good Shepherd, crowned the Head of Wisdom Incarnate, and still went on doing it, they would never have been saved. They would have been damned! It was only their ignorance which brought them within the pale of redemption and forgiveness. As St. Peter told them on Pentecost: "I know that you did it through ignorance: as did also your rulers." *(Acts 3:17).*

Why is it that you and I, for example, can sin a thousand times and be forgiven, and the angels who have sinned but once are eternally unforgiven? The reason is that the angels *knew* what they were doing. The angels see the consequences of each and every one of their decisions with the same clarity that you see that a part can never be greater than the whole. Once you make that judgment you can never take it back. It is irrevocable; it is eternal.

Now the angels saw the consequences of their choices with still greater clarity. Therefore, when they made a decision, they made it knowingly and there was no taking it back. They were lost forever. Tremendous are the responsibilities of knowing! Those who know the truth will be judged more severely than those who know it not. As Our Blessed Lord said: "If I had not come...they would not have sin" *(John 15:22)*.

The First Word Our Blessed Mother spoke at the Annunciation revealed the same lesson. She said: "I know not man." Why was there a value in not knowing man? Because she had consecrated her virginity to God. At a moment when every woman sought the privilege of being the mother of the Messiah, Mary gave up the hope and received it. She refuses to discuss with an angel any kind of compromise with her high resolve.

If the condition of becoming the Mother of God was the surrender of her vow, she would not make that surrender, knowing man would have been evil for her, though it would not have been evil in other circumstances. Not knowing man is a kind of ignorance, but here it proves to be such a blessing that in an instant the Holy Spirit overshadows her, making her a living ciborium privileged to bear within herself for nine months the Guest Who is the Host of the World.

These first words of Jesus and Mary suggest there is value in not knowing evil. You live in a world in which the worldly wise say: "You do not know life; you have never lived." They assume that you can know nothing except by experience -- experience not only of good but of evil.

It was with this kind of lie that Satan tempted our First Parents. He told them that the reason God forbade them to eat of the tree of the knowledge of good and evil was because God did not want them to be wise as He was wise. Satan did not tell them that if they came to a knowledge of good and evil, it would be very different from God's knowledge.

God knows evil only abstractly, i.e., by negation of His Goodness and Love. But man would know it concretely and experimentally, and thus would to some extent fall captive to the very evil which he experienced. God wanted our First Parents to know typhoid fever, for example, as a healthy doctor knows it; he did not want them to know it as the stricken patient knows it. And from that day of the Great Lie, down to this, no one is better because he knows evil through experience.

Examine your own life. If you know evil by experience, are you wiser because of it? Have you not despised that very evil and are you not the more tragic for having experienced it? You may even have become mastered by the evil you experienced. How often the disillusioned say: "I wish I had never tasted liquor" or "I regret the day I stole my first dollar," and "I wish I had never known that person." How much wiser you would have been had you been ignorant!

Over and over again, when you broke some law which you thought arbitrary and meaningless, you discovered the principle which dictated it. As a child, you could not understand why your parents forbade you to play with matches, but the burn convinced you of the truth of the law. So the world by violating God's moral law is finding through war, strife, and misery the wisdom of the law. How it would now like to unlearn its false learning!

Think not, then, that in order to "know life" you must "experience evil." Is a doctor wiser because he is prostrate with disease? Do we know cleanliness by living in sewers? Do we know education by experiencing stupidity? Do we know peace by fighting? Do we know the joys of vision by being blinded? Do you become a better pianist by hitting the wrong keys? You do not need to get drunk to know what drunkenness is.

Do not excuse yourself by saying, "temptations are too strong" or "good people do not know what temptation is." The good know more about the strength of temptations than those who fall. How do you know how strong the current of a river is? By swimming with the current or by swimming against it? How do you know how strong the enemy is in battle? By being captured or by conquering? How can you know the strength of a temptation unless you overcome it? Our Blessed Lord really understands the power of temptation better than anyone, because He overcame the temptations of Satan.

The great fallacy of modern education is the assumption that the reason there is evil in the world is because there is ignorance, and that if we pour more facts in the minds of the young we will make them better. If this were true, we should be the most virtuous people in the history of the world, because we are the best educated.

The facts, however, point the other way: Never before has there been so much education and never before so little coming to the knowledge of the truth. We forget that ignorance is better than error. *Scientia* is not *sapientia*. Much of modern education is making the mind sceptical about the wisdom of God. The young are not born sceptics, but a false education can make them sceptical. The modern world is dying of sceptic poisoning.

The fallacy of sex education is assuming that if children know the evil effects of certain acts, they will abstain from those acts. It is argued that if you knew there was typhoid fever in a house you would not go into that house. But what these educators forget is that sex-appeal is not at all like the typhoid fever appeal. No person has an urge to break down the doors of a typhoid patient, but the same cannot be said about sex. There is a sex-impulse, but there is no typhoid instinct.

Sex wisdom does not necessarily make one wise; it can make one desire the evil, particularly when we learn that the evil effects can be avoided. Sex Hygiene is not morality. Soap is not the same as virtue. Badness comes not from our ignorance of knowing, but from our perversity of doing.

That is why in our Catholic schools, we train and discipline the will as well as inform the intellect, because we know that character is in our choices, not in our knowing. All of us already *know* enough to be good, even before we start to school. What we have to learn is how to *do better*.

If we forget the burden of our fallen nature, and the accumulated proneness to evil that comes from submitting to it, we soon become chained as Samson was and all the education in the world cannot break those chains. Education may conceivably rationalize the chains and make us believe they are charms, but only the effort of the will plus the grace of God can free us from their servitude. Without those two energies we will never do one jot or tittle beyond that which we have already done.

Train your children and yourself, then, in the true wisdom which is the knowledge of God, and in the ignorance of the things that are evil. The unknown is the undesired; to be ignorant of wickedness is not to desire it. There are no joys like Innocence.

Here on the Cross and on its shadow were the two most Innocent Persons of all history: Jesus was absolutely sinless because He is the Son of God; Mary was Immaculate because she was preserved free from original sin, in virtue of the merits of her Divine Son. It was their innocence which made their sufferings so keen.

People living in dirt hardly ever realize how dirty dirt is. Those who live in sin hardly understand the horror of sin. The one peculiar and terrifying thing about sin is that the more experience you have with it, the less you know about it. You become so identified with it that you know neither the depths to which you have sunk nor the heights from which you have fallen.

You never know you were asleep until you wake up, and you never know the horror of sin until you get out of sin. Hence, only the sinless really know what sin is. And since here on the Cross and beneath it, there is Innocence at its highest, it follows that there was also the greatest sorrow. Since there was no sin, there was the greatest understanding of its evil. It was their innocence, or their ignorance of evil, which made the agonies of Calvary.

To Jesus Who forgave those who "know not," to Mary who won God because she could say "I know not," pray that you may know not evil and thus be good.

Honestly, if you had the choice now either of learning more about the world, or of unlearning the evil you know, would you not rather unlearn than learn? Would you not be better if you were stripped of your wickedness than if you were clothed in the sheepskin of diplomas?

Would you not like to be right now, just as you came from the hands of God at the baptismal font, with no worldly wisdom yet gathered to your mind, so that like an empty chalice, you might spend your life filling it with the wine of His Love? The world would call you ignorant, saying you knew nothing about life. Do not believe it -- you would have Life! Therefore you would be one of the wisest persons in the world.

There is so much error in the world today, there are such vast areas of experienced and lived evil, that it would be a blessing if some generous soul would endow a University for Unlearning. Its purpose would be to do with error and evil exactly what doctors do with disease.

Would you be surprised to know that Our Lord did actually institute such a University for Unlearning, and to it all devout Catholics go about once a month? It is called the confessional! You will not be given a sheepskin when you walk out of that confessional, but you will feel like a lamb because Christ is your Shepherd. You will be amazed at how much you will learn by unlearning. It is easier for God to write on a blank page than on one covered with your scribblings.

Seven Words Of Jesus And Mary, 1945

Acknowledgments

To the Archbishop Fulton John Sheen Foundation in Peoria, Illinois for there help and encouragement in the creation of this book series on the Seven Last Words.

We would also like to acknowledge the Most Rev. Daniel R. Jenky, C.S.C., Bishop of Peoria, in appreciation for his many years of leadership and fidelity to Archbishop Sheen's cause for canonization.

www.archbishopsheencause.org

To the staff at Sophia Institute Press for their invaluable assistance. Their mission to nurture the spiritual, moral and cultural life of souls and to spread the gospel of Christ in conformity with the authentic teachings of the Roman Catholic Church is very much appreciated.

www.sophiainstitute.com

To the good folks at Bishop Sheen Today. We value your guidance, support, and prayers in helping us to share the wisdom of Archbishop Fulton J. Sheen with a whole new generation of readers. Your apostolic work of sharing his audio and video presentations along with his many writings to a worldwide audience is very much appreciated.

www.bishopsheentoday.com

And lastly, to Archbishop Fulton J. Sheen, whose teachings on the Holy Hour and prayer continue to inspire many to love God more and to appreciate the gift of the Church. May we be so blessed as to imitate Archbishop Sheen's love for the saints, the sacraments, the Eucharist, and the Blessed Virgin Mary. May the Good Lord grant him a very high place in heaven!

About the Author

Fulton J. Sheen
(1895–1979)

Archbishop Sheen, best known for his popularly televised and syndicated television program, Life is Worth Living, is held today as one of Catholicism's most widely recognized figures of the twentieth century.

Fulton John Sheen, born May 8, 1895 in El Paso, Illinois was raised and educated in the Roman Catholic faith. Originally named Peter John Sheen, he came to be known as a young boy by his mother's maiden name, Fulton. Over the course of many dedicated, steadfast years, he was ordained a priest of the Diocese of Peoria at St. Mary's Cathedral in Peoria, IL on September 20, 1919.

Following his ordination, Sheen moved overseas to further his education, and earned a doctorate in Philosophy from The Catholic University of Louvain in Belgium in 1923. That same year, he received the Cardinal Mercier Prize for International Philosophy, becoming the first ever American to earn this distinction.

Upon returning to America after varied and extensive work throughout Europe, Sheen continued to preach, as well as teach theology and philosophy at the Catholic University of America in Washington DC from 1927 until 1950.

Starting in 1930, Sheen became a host on a weekly Sunday night radio broadcast called The Catholic Hour. This broadcast captured many devoted listeners, reportedly drawing an audience of four million people every week for two decades.

In 1950, he became the National Director of the Society for the Propagation of the Faith, raising money to support the missions. During the 16 years that he held this position, he raised millions of dollars to support the missionary activity of the Church. These efforts influenced tens of millions of people all over the world, bringing them to know Christ and his Church. In addition, his own preaching and personal example brought about many converts to Catholicism.

In 1951, Sheen was appointed Auxiliary Bishop of the Archdiocese of New York. That same year, Sheen moved from his weekly radio broadcast to hosting the Catholic television program, Life is Worth Living. This show aired every Tuesday evening at 8pm for six years.

Over the course of the show, Sheen's Life is Worth Living competed for airtime with popular television stars such as Frank Sinatra and Milton Berle. Sheen's show held its own, and in 1953, just two years after its debut, he won an Emmy Award for "Most Outstanding Television Personality." Fulton Sheen credited the Gospel writers - Matthew, Mark, Luke, and John - for their valuable contribution to his success. This television show ran until 1957, boasting as many as 30 million weekly viewers.

In the fall of 1966, Sheen was appointed Bishop of Rochester, New York. During this time, Bishop Sheen hosted another television series, The Fulton Sheen Program; running from 1961 to 1968 that closely modeled the Life is Worth Living series.

After nearly three years as Bishop of Rochester, Fulton Sheen resigned and was appointed the Archbishop of Titular See of Newport Wales by Pope Paul VI. This new appointment allowed Sheen the flexibility to continue preaching.

Sheen was known for his annual Good Friday homilies that he preached for 58 consecutive years in New York and elsewhere. Sheen also led numerous retreats for priests and religious, and preached at conferences all over the world.

When asked by Pope Pius XII how many converts he had made, Sheen responded, "Your Holiness, I have never counted them. I am always afraid if I did count them, I might think I made them, instead of the Lord."

"If you want people to stay as they are," he said, "tell them what they want to hear. If you want to improve them, tell them what they should know." This he did, not only in his preaching but also in the numerous books and articles he wrote. His book entitled 'Peace of Soul' was sixth on the New York Times best-seller list.

Three of Sheen's great loves were for the Missions and the propagation of the faith; the Blessed Mother; and the Eucharist.

He made a daily holy hour before the Blessed Sacrament, from which he drew strength and inspiration to preach the gospel and in the presence of which he prepared his homilies. "I beg [Christ] every day to keep me strong physically and alert mentally in order to preach His gospel and proclaim His Cross and Resurrection," he said. "I am so happy doing this that I sometimes feel that when I come to the good Lord in Heaven, I will take a few days' rest and then ask Him to allow me to come back again to this earth to do some more work."

His contributions to the Catholic Church are numerous and varied, ranging from educating in classrooms, churches, and homes, to preaching over a nationally publicized radio show, and two television programs, as well as penning over 50 written works. Bishop Fulton J. Sheen had a gift for communicating the Word of God in the most pure, simple way. His strong background in philosophy helped him to relate to all of his followers in a highly personalized manner. His timeless messages continue to have great relevance today. He inspires each of us to live a God-centered life with the joy and love that God intended.

On October 2, 1979 Archbishop Sheen received his greatest accolade when Pope John Paul II embraced him at St. Patrick's Cathedral in New York City. The Holy Father said to him, "You have written and spoken well of the Lord Jesus. You are a loyal son of the Church."

The Good Lord called Fulton Sheen home on December 9, 1979. His television broadcasts, now on tape, and his books continue his earthly work of winning souls for Christ. Sheen's cause for canonization was opened in 2002 and in 2012, Pope Benedict XVI declared him "Venerable." In July of 2019, Pope Francis formally approved the miracle that is attributed to the intercession of the Venerable Archbishop Fulton J. Sheen. This announcement allows a beatification ceremony to take place in the future. The time and date for the church to declare Archbishop Fulton J. Sheen a saint is in God's hands.

Bibliography Notes

(First Meditation) - Fulton J. Sheen, The Seven Last Words – (New York: Century Co. Ltd., 1933), pp. 3-9.

(Second Meditation) - Fulton J. Sheen, The Fullness of Christ – (Huntington, IN: Our Sunday Visitor, 1935), pp. 147.

(Third Meditation) - Fulton J. Sheen, Calvary And The Mass – (New York: P.J. Kenedy & Sons, 1936), pp. 17-26

(Fourth Meditation) - Fulton J. Sheen, The Cross And The Beatitudes, - (New York: P.J. Kenedy & Sons, 1937), pp. 3-18.

(Fifth Meditation) - Fulton J. Sheen, The Rainbow of Sorrow - (New York: P.J. Kenedy & Sons 1938), pp. 3-19.

(Sixth Meditation) - Fulton J. Sheen, Victory Over Vice – (New York: P.J. Kenedy & Sons, 1939), pp. 1-12.

(Seventh Meditation) - Fulton J. Sheen, The Seven Virtues - (New York: P.J. Kenedy & Sons, 1940), pp. 3-25.

(Eighth Meditation) - Fulton J. Sheen, Seven Words To The Cross – (New York: P.J. Kenedy & Sons, 1944), pp. 11-21.

(Ninth Meditation) - Fulton J. Sheen, Seven Words of Jesus and Mary - (New York: P.J. Kenedy & Sons, 1945), pp. 13-29.

On The Front Cover

Jesus and the Thieves – A Painting by Michael O'Brien (2008)

Artist Commentary: Jesus promises Paradise to the repentant thief. We tend to think that when severe trials come we will suffer with the same courage and love as Jesus did. Or, perhaps as the "good thief" did. Yet we often find ourselves reacting to trials in the manner of the unrepentant thief. Within our hearts is the potential for all three responses. In life's difficulties, we are refined and tested, our hearts are revealed to us, that we might turn and turn again to the One who died for us on the Cross. If we do not succumb to bitterness or despair, or run from what we must learn, we will be with Him "this day in Paradise."